Wandering Woman: Michigan

The Ultimate Road Trip: One Woman's
Journey Across the United States by RV

Julie Bettendorf

Contents

Introduction

"Not all who wander are lost." JRR Tolkien

Are you sure? I thought to myself, as I tried not to panic. I was a long way from anything familiar, but that was how it should be. I had driven thousands of miles on dusty, pothole-filled roads. It's often on the worst roads that you can discover something truly amazing.

My dusty CRV was parked beside me, containing one restless dog and a variety of snack bags, all empty by now. There were no buildings in sight, no cars or people or movement at all. Only the constant humming of the insects as they buzzed around my head.

I turned to my left – another straight road that trailed off into the distance. I glanced over to the right, then behind me – two more barely discernible roads stretched out into the abyss. I was in a four-way intersection with no signs, no sense of direction, and no sign of life for several miles. No cell service either. *Damn*, I thought. *I'm lost*.

How did I get here? I couldn't help but feel like this little intersection was a cruel metaphor for life. I began to daydream, imagining each road might transport me back to a different time, a different role in my life, and a different me.

If I took the road from whence I came, it could lead me all the way back to Oregon, back to my cheating third husband, back to a life of loneliness and solitude. There is no greater loneliness than being married to someone who isn't actually present in your life.

If I took the road to my left, perhaps it could take me back to my career as a dental hygienist, a job I hated deep down in my soul. There is something so disengaging about cleaning teeth for a living. It's a disgusting, smelly way to get a paycheck. It pays well, which is great, but the best part is the huge gob of friends I enjoy to this day.

Or maybe the road to my right, *yes – maybe that's the path*, I imagined. Maybe it could take me back to my real treasure, my kids. Back to their smiling, innocent faces as toddlers, as they danced around the Christmas tree and their father and I were still married. Back when they still needed me for every little thing.

But, that was just it. I didn't feel needed anymore. My kids weren't toddlers anymore – they were both full-grown adults, and far too busy for me. My dental buddies were still working, but I wasn't. Dental hygiene had robbed me of the cartilage in my fingers, giving me severe, disabling arthritis. And, I wouldn't be returning to any more husbands either, because three marriages were quite enough for me.

All three of these paths, all three of these roles – the wife, the mother, and the dental hygienist – had seemingly been stripped from me within a year. I was lost and looking to find myself again.

The funny thing about this phrase, "not all who wander are lost" – is that, in my experience, wandering and being lost walk hand-in-hand with one another, and the expression can be flipped. In my experience, not all who are lost are wandering, and that is a real disservice to the beauty and clarity that the world has to offer.

When one becomes lost, wandering is the only option to guide oneself back to a path. After all, one could not come upon any dirt path at all without wandering.

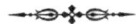

I began wandering at an early age, both with my mind and with my feet. At eight years old, I was reading a book about archaeology and dreaming of one day seeing Egypt. I didn't follow a traditional path in high school either, going heavily into foreign languages, in hopes of one day using them.

At twenty-five years old, I divorced my first husband (the dental student who talked me into becoming a dental hygienist so I could work for him) and decided to give traveling a real shot. I took off for the Andes and Macchu Picchu, climbing up ancient Inca stone steps to reach the magnificent ruins.

Anyone who has been to Macchu Picchu will tell you there is something ethereal and deeply spiritual about the place. The ruins stretch out across the emerald green mountains, way up in the middle of the sky. Macchu Picchu gave me my first experience of feeling history. This trip inspired me to come back and complete a degree in archaeology, and I've been wandering ever since.

More travel followed including a backpack trip around Europe for three months, by myself, and trips to Britain, Italy, and Greece. I visited the burial places of Crusaders, mummies, and ancient kings. I happened upon the castle of my namesake in Bettendorf, Luxembourg, and wandered my way through European history.

My favorite excursion by far was finally seeing Egypt with my daughter in 2012. Just like my childhood dream envisioned, I rode a camel beneath the pyramids of Giza, with my head wrapped in some man's sweaty turban. It was perfect.

Traveling has always been my own personal antidote to pain. I went to Mexico after my first and second divorces, Canada after my third, and Italy after my dad died. Call it avoidance if you want, but I call it an accelerated form of healing in the purest sense of the word. I believe travel can heal your soul.

Wandering has always worked its wonders on me – made me feel renewed, rejoiceful, grateful, and purposeful. It's been my medicine.

So, as I stood in that intersection, I once again wondered how wandering had led me so astray this time. *What the hell am I supposed to do now?* It was then that I realized that one last path had not been considered yet – the path which stretched straight out in front of me. *Which role does this represent?* I pondered.

The answer smacked me in the face.

That last dirt road – the only path that could take me where I wanted to go, the only path that ever truly healed me or showed me the way – was the path of the traveler. The wife, the mother, and the hygienist roles – though valued in their time – were sitting in the bleachers now. It was time to welcome and enable my boldest, bravest, and perhaps most pivotal role yet:

The role of the Wandering Woman.

Welcome to Wandering Woman

This book is for you – the grieving empty nester mom, the begrudged housewife, the woman in need of a drastic change in her life. Really, this book is for anyone with a passion for traveling. If you feel lost with no sense of direction or purpose in life, that's a bonus – this book will be even more appealing to you. And lastly, if you're a man reading this book, congratulations for holding a book with the word woman in the title. You're contributing to gender equality, and that's pretty neat.

I decided to combine three of my dearest loves – travel, history, and archaeology – and put them into a book because I believe wandering has the power to change your life. I have been to many areas of the world and have enjoyed too many outstanding experiences to list. However, by the time both my children moved out in 2017, I realized I was a stranger in my own country. It was the perfect time to explore a new country (my own) and discover a new me at the same time. I have been traveling for five years now, and I've upgraded to a small RV. I also have a new traveling companion, another sweet Sheltie, named Rosie. *Wandering Woman* is the chronicle of my journey across the United States, discovering the joy of getting lost and finding myself along the way.

Why You Need to Take a Road Trip

A merica, the beautiful? I sure think so, but I didn't realize just how beautiful our country is until I embarked on traveling across the United States, full time, in a small RV.

The United States offers something for everyone. From spectacular beaches, austere mountains, to rolling plains, our country has it all. It's difficult to comprehend just how large and impressive our scenery is, until you experience it first-hand, with the ultimate road trip.

I also realized just how much of our history is missing from U.S. history I was taught as a kid. The history of our country didn't begin with the pilgrims landing on Plymouth Rock in the 1600s. Our history is far more ancient, with rock art and archaeological sites dating back over 12,000 years.

We owe a tremendous debt to early pioneers who tamed our land. The Mormons and other groups ventured into the great unknown with their families and their worldly possessions. Some of them pulled cumbersome handcarts across the country to settle in inhospitable, dangerous locations.

The goal of **Wandering Woman** is to bring history back to life and make it interesting again. I am presenting some famous sites, and many little-known ones. You will take the road-less-traveled with me, while we explore ghost towns, rock art sites, archaeological sites, and museums, to discover the colorful tapestry that is our country.

I present some history, including dates, but my goal is to present more of the real-life stories of history, including ghost stories, profiles in history, voices from the past, and moments in time, to give you, the reader, a deeper understanding of the context of history.

This is by no means an exhaustive list of places to visit. In fact, I encourage you to discover America for yourself, as I am doing, by making a trek across the land by car or RV. You can venture forth as the early explorers did, just a little more comfortably, with a lot less hardship.

I hope you enjoy this book and take a little time out to discover our beautiful country, and maybe even discover yourself in the process.

Safe Travels,

Julie Bettendorf

Welcome to Michigan

The Great Lakes State

*M*ichigan is uniquely charming. From Mackinac Island to Old Victoria, the Upper Peninsula offers a glimpse into the past. Michigan is also the center of industrialization, thanks to Henry Ford and the automobile. There is a lot to love about

Michigan, from the rugged coastline to the fascinating historical sites, to the warm, welcoming Michiganders. Michigan is waiting to be explored.

5 Things to Love about Michigan:

- World-class museums like the Henry Ford Museum of American Innovation

- The rugged, spectacular coastline of the Upper Peninsula

- Earling mining history from places like Fayette and Quincy Mine

- Early military history from places like Fort Mackinac

- The many picturesque lighthouses that border the Great Lakes

Dreams of Michigan

"I think Michigan keeps you sane and on an even keel through the ups and downs. In Michigan, I do fireworks, shovel snow and live life." *Jeff Daniels*

"The first thing to know about playing baseball in Michigan is, Michigan's really cold." *Derek Jeter*

"I think I was 9, and my mom ordered them for me from a catalogue. They bred like crazy, and I was selling gerbils all around Michigan. They wrote a story about me in the local newspaper." *K. A. Applegate*

Famous People from Michigan

Charles Lindbergh, aviator, (1902 - 1974)

Henry Ford, automaker, (1863 – 1947)

Rosa Parks, civil rights activist, (1913-2005)

Ken Burns, author & film maker, (born 1953)

Jerry Bruckheimer, film maker, (born 1943)

Aretha Franklin, singer, (1942 – 2018)

Madonna, singer, (born 1958)

Serena Williams, athlete, (born 1981)

Gerald R. Ford, 38th president of the U.S. (1913 – 2006)

Early Michigan

Early Fayette

Early Victoria

Old Mackinac Lighthouse

River Raisin Battlefield

The ***River Raisin National Battlefield Park*** is the site of the Battle of Frenchtown, the only national battlefield from the War of 1812. From January 18th through January 23rd, 1813, fierce conflict took place here, along the River Raisin.

Initially, the Americans were successful at repelling the British Army. The combined forces of the British and Native Americans later overcame the American forces on the 22nd of January.

397 Americans died, and 547 were taken prisoner by the British Army. It was the worst American defeat during the war.

In 2000, scattered human remains were found indicating what may have been the main skirmish line of the battle. The remains were reburied in several sites in the area.

How to get to River Raisin Battlefield:

The River Raisin National Battlefield Park is located at 333 N. Dixie Hwy, in Monroe, Michigan.

A moment in time:

On the morning of January 23, 1813, after the battle, the American soldiers who could walk were marched off toward Fort Malden. The wounded soldiers unable to walk were housed in two buildings, with no one left to care for them. Later that morning, a group of Native Americans came back and began to kill the wounded soldiers and set fire to the buildings. The exact number of dead is unknown, but is estimated to be between 30 and 100 soldiers. This event is known as the ***River Raisin Massacre.*** The massacre was especially difficult for Kentucky, the state which supplied many of the soldiers who were lost in the battle.

Voices from the past:

"I saw the Indians take off several prisoners whom I afterwards saw in the road, in a most mangled condition, and entirely stripped of their clothing...an Indian came up to one Mr. Searls... The Indian then raised his tomahawk and struck him on the shoulder which cut into the cavity of the body. Searls then caught hold of the tomahawk and appeared to resist and upon my telling that his fate was inevitable, he closed his eyes and received the savage blow which terminated his existence. I was near enough to him to receive the brains and blood, after that fatal blow on my blanket. A short time after the death of Searls, I saw three others share a similar fate." **Surgeon's mate Gustavus Bower.**

Henry Ford's Museum of American Innovation

H *enry Ford's Museum of American Innovation* is a must-see museum. You don't have to be a car person to love this place. Henry Ford was a collector, beginning his collection in 1906. He used his millions to amass an incredible collection of American memorabilia that tells our story.

When you enter this fantastic museum, you will enjoy historic automobiles, including Franklin Delano Roosevelt's 1939 Lincoln.

Another presidential automobile within the museum is Dwight Eisenhower's 1950 Lincoln.

You will also see John F. Kennedy's 1961 Lincoln Continental which he was riding in when he was assassinated on November 22, 1963.

There are thousands of artifacts representing America's history. One of my favorite pieces is a powder horn from 1775 Massachusetts. The figure on the horse is believed to be George Washington.

Other pieces from George Washington's time including his folding camp bed, from 1775-1780, and Washington's camp chest from 1783.

There are also several pieces in the museum representing sad events in America's history. One of these pieces is fhe chair from Ford's Theatre Lincoln was sitting in when he was shot.

Don't miss the bus Rosa Parks was sitting in when she was arrested on December 1, 1955. The seat she sat in is clearly marked in the exhibit.

How to get to the Ford Museum:

The Ford Museum is located at 20900 Oakwood Blvd, in Dearborn.

Profiles in history:

Rosa Parks was born in Tuskegee, Alabama on February 4, 1913. She grew up under the strict segregation of the Jim Crow era. Rosa moved to Montgomery, Alabama, and joined the NAACP as a secretary. It was the custom in Montgomery for black patrons to give up seats in the front of the bus to white patrons. The back rows of the bus were designated for black patrons.

On December 1, 1955, Rosa boarded a bus at 5:30, and seated herself in the middle section, next to a black man and across from two black women. All the white-only seats began to fill up. The bus driver demanded the black passengers seated in the middle rows give up their seats. The black passengers seated near her gave up their seats, but Rosa remained seated. The bus driver called the police, and Rosa was arrested. Parks' bail was paid and she was released. Rosa Parks became an icon of Civil Rights for Black

Americans. She died on October 24, 2005, of natural causes. Rosa Parks was 92 years old.

Henry Ford was born on July 30, 1863, in a farmhouse in Spring-wells Township, Michigan. At 16, Ford left his childhood home to find work in Detroit. He eventually came to work for Edison Electric in 1891, and later founded the Ford Motor Company in 1903. In addition to developing a self-propelled automobile, Ford was a champion for workers. In 1914, he offered a daily wage of $5, which is the equivalent of $157 in 2024. Ford also was a pioneer in creating work/life balance by establishing the 5, 8-hour day workweek. Henry Ford died on April 7, 1947, from a cerebral hemorrhage.

Voices from the past:

"I am collecting the history of our people as written into things their hands made and used .... When we are through, we shall have reproduced American life as lived, and that, I think, is the best way of preserving at least a part of our history and tradition." **Henry Ford**

Greenfield Village

*G**reenfield Village*** is the wonderful outdoor museum next to the Henry Ford Museum of American Innovation, and was the first outdoor museum of its kind in the country.

The village contains about one hundred historical buildings which were moved there. Buildings from the 1600s to the present are in the village.

One of my favorite buildings is a replica of Thomas Edison's laboratory complex from New Jersey. The buildings incorporate exact measurements of the foundations of Edison's original laboratory.

When you step inside, you will enjoy both original and replica artifacts contained in the original laboratory.

Another interesting building is the original Wright brothers bicycle shop and home, which were moved from Dayton, Ohio, by Henry Ford in 1937.

In 1899. the Wright brothers began their research about building an airplane in this building. They closed their bicycle shop in 1904 to begin work on their airplanes.

There is also a wonderful replica of the Ford Motor Company Building, which is one-third the size of the original building. Ford began constructing early vehicles in 1903.

I also enjoyed Dr. Howard's Office, a cozy little red building, occupied by Dr. Alonson Howard from 1852 to 1883.

He used a combination of plants, herbs, and traditional medicine of the time to treat his patients in the home.

Don't miss the sobering Hermitage Slave Quarters, one of 52 slave quarters at the Hermitage.

201 slaves were housed at the Hermitage plantation in Georgia in 1850. This building was constructed about 1820.

How to get to Greenfield Village:

Greenfield Village is located next to Henry Ford's Museum of American Innovation in Dearborn.

Voices from the past:

"Mother instructed my sister to run away...Mrs. Cox sent for my mother and told her that Nancy had run away. Outwardly she pretended to be angry. In her heart arose a prayer of thanksgiving." **Lucy A. Delaney, 1890**

"My father must join his master and go west....My mother and father never met again. They kept up correspondence for years. In every letter was a message to me..." **Elizabeth Keckley, 1868**

Profiles in history:

Thomas Edison was born in Milan, Ohio, in 1847. In 1854, his family moved to Port Huron, Michigan, where Edison grew up. With only three months of education, he became an inventor, eventually acquiring 1093 patents in his lifetime. Some of his most famous inventions include the light bulb, sound recording, motion pictures, and alkaline batteries. Edison died on October 18, 1931.

Voices from the past:

"I never did anything by accident, nor did any of my inventions come by accident. They came by work." **Thomas Edison**

Sanilac Petroglyphs

T he *Sanilac Petroglyphs* are famous for a large sandstone mound, containing about 165 petroglyphs. Settlers found the petroglyphs after a massive forest fire occurred in 1881.

The exact date of the petroglyphs is unknown, but they are believed to have been carved between 300 and 1400 years ago.

One of the most famous of the petroglyphs is that of Ebmodaakowet, the archer, believed to be able to shoot knowledge into the future.

Stone tools and artifacts have been found in the park.

The area surrounding the petroglyphs has been inhabited for about 8,000 years.

How to get to Sanilac Petroglyphs:

The Sanilac Petroglyphs are located at 8251 Germania Rd, in Cass City, Michigan

Fayette Historic Park

F*ayette Historic State Park* is the site of the town of
Fayette. It's a beautiful spot, on the shores of Lake Michigan.
Fayette was founded in the late 1860s by Fayette Brown, manager
of the Jackson Iron Company.

Nearly 230,000 tons of iron were produced at Fayette, to be used for railroad rails and steel products.

At its peak, Fayette boasted a band, baseball team, horse racing track, school, post office, hotel, and store.

The town began to decline when the Jackson Iron Company closed in 1891.

Today, you can visit twenty buildings, including the furnaces, employee housing, and the business district.

The Jackson Iron Company Hotel, known as The Shelton House, was fitted out with Brussels carpets, marble-topped tables, silver eating utensils, and fine decor.

To stay in the hotel, laborers paid 15 cents per night for a single bed, or 10 cents per night for a double. Guests on the property paid $1.50 to $2.00 per night.

The Company Pay Office was home to an accountant who doled out an average of $5,826 each month, which was divided up among 153 employees.

Don't miss the "Doctor's House" on the outskirts of the town site. The house interprets the residence of Dr. Curtis J. Bellows, who came to Fayette in 1870 to practice medicine after the Civil War.

Upstairs in the Doctor's House, you can see how a kitchen and parlor from the 1880s might have looked.

As you wander the beautiful grounds of Fayette, be on the lookout for curious wildlife.

How to get to Fayette Historic Park:

Fayette Historic Park is located at 4785 II Road, in Garden, Michigan.

Old Victoria

*O**ld Victoria*** began in 1843, when a large copper boulder, weighing 3708 pounds, was removed from the area. The boulder is now in the Smithsonian. Thus began the Victoria Mining Company, established in 1858.

Initial production wasn't much, and so the mine was revamped in 1899. 20 log homes and 50 frame houses were built to house the miners.

Victoria Mine once employed 250 people, many of whom were immigrants. Married men and their families lived in the frame houses, and single men lived in the log houses, some of which were boarding houses. A boardinghouse typically housed a family downstairs and up to a dozen boarders upstairs.

The mine closed down in 1921, and many of the houses were torn down. Four log homes in their original locations can be visited today. Salvage materials from the 1899 cabins were used in the reconstruction.

I was told by the caretaker that the earliest settlers came to the area in the 1770s.

Old Victoria ghost town contains the four log buildings, complete with furnishings of the period. It's a beautiful spot, nestled in trees and emerald green grass. It's a nice way to spend a few hours.

How to get to Old Victoria:

Old Victoria is located at 25401 Victoria Dam Road, about 4 miles from Rockland, MI.

Ghost story:

Miners who worked at the Victoria Copper Mining Company lived at Old Victoria. At least 25 men died in the mine, and women and children died of illness, childbirth, and other causes. In 1911, Johanna Arvola died after suffering a miscarriage. She was 39 years old. Witnesses speak of a rocking chair which will begin rocking on its own in the Arvola house. This is believed to be the ghost of Johanna rocking her unborn baby.

There is another ghost in Old Victoria. It's that of a miner with a lantern, walking up to the remains of his house. Half of the apparition's face is missing. This ghost is believed to be that of a miner killed in an explosion.

Hanka Homestead

The *Hanka Homestead* was built in 1896 by Hjalmer Hanka, using hand tools, and with a little help from his neighbors. The homestead is located in an area known as Askel, which means "step" in Finnish.

The grounds contain the family house, a wonderful two-story home, with a well next to it, which was dug by hand.

Other buildings at the site include the blacksmith shop, where Hanka shoed horses, made metal tools, and created bicycle parts. There is also a large barn which could house six horses and their feed.

Crops including vegetables and grains were grown, and cattle, horses, pigs, and chickens were raised to feed the Hanka family.

The smoke sauna, which is an important part of Finnish culture, often had several functions, including social meetings, birthing babies, smoking meats, and cupping, which was the medical treatment for drawing blood, and preparing the dead. Hanka Homestead Historical Site

How to get to Hanka Homestead:

The Hanka Homestead Museum is located 6 miles west of US HWY 41 off Tower Road, in Pelkie.

Quincy Mine

The **Quincy Mine** was established in 1848, to mine the extensive copper deposits of the Keweenaw area. It was the most successful copper mine during the 1840s. The mine was named after the town of Quincy, Massachusetts, which invested in the mine.

The Quincy Mine supplied and maintained housing for the workers, ranging from tents to three-story houses later on. The houses often lacked electricity and running water.

Today you can visit the Miner's Memorial House, containing furniture and artifacts from the period.

Copper was in high demand for ammunition during the Civil War, and dividends were paid out regularly to investors from 1862 to 1920. The Quincy Mine soon earned the nickname of "Old Reliable."

After almost 100 years, Quincy stopped operations in 1945.

As you walk around the Quincy Mine, you can visit several build-ings, including the Supply Office, built in 1893, which now houses the gift shop. Other buildings include the old No. 2 hoist house, in use from 1882 to 1894, and the ruins of North Quincy dry house, from before 1890.

How to get to the Quincy Mine:

The Quincy mine is located at 49750 US Hwy 41, in Hancock.

Ghost story:

There is a legend about ***Tommyknockers*** that are said to haunt many mining camps. Tommyknockers got their name from Cornish miners who believed that little men lived underground and caused the knocking with their tiny hammers.

Some early miners believed Tommyknockers were good spirits who were warning of an impending mine collapse. Others believed that the person who heard the knocking would die. Still others believed that Tommyknockers were the spirits of miners who had died during a cave-in. Some miners even left offerings of food and drink to appease the Tommyknockers.

Calumet

The beautiful city of *Calumet* was settled in 1864 and originally called Red Jacket, after a Seneca Chief. The town became Calumet in 1929.

Calumet is famous for rich copper mines. The Calumet and Hecla Mining Companies were established, producing over half the the country's copper from 1871 through 1880. Calumet's population declined after the Copper Country Strike of 1913 and 1914.

As you walk around this beautiful town, don't miss the Calumet Theatre, which opened in 1900.

The theatre was state-of-the-art, containing an electrified copper chandelier, and an ornate ceiling.

Another interesting building is St. Paul the Apostle Church, established in 1889 by Slovenian immigrants. The church cost $100,000 to build.

Calumet winters were difficult, accumulating snow up to 300 inches each year. Snow was pushed aside by huge snowplows powered by steam locomotives.

How to get to Calumet:

Calumet is located on Michigan's Upper Peninsula, 30 miles south of Copper Harbor.

A moment in time:

The ***Italian Hall Disaster*** in Calumet occurred on Christmas Eve, in 1913. Hundreds of people, including miners and their families, were gathered in the Italian Hall for a holiday celebration. An unknown person yelled "fire" causing panic in the building. There was only a narrow stairway, leading down from the upper level, and a fire escape which had to be accessed through a window. As a result, 73 people, including 59 children, were crushed to death, It turns out, there was no fire at all.

Fort Wilkins

*F*ort Wilkins Historic State Park* is in a lovely spot, bordering Lake Superior. The fort was established by the army in 1844, to guard against unrest from the incoming flood of copper miners and the Ojibwa tribe, native to the area.

Fort Wilkins also became the focus of shipping supplies to the area, and shipping copper out.

The fort originally contained 27 structures including a guardhouse, officer's quarters, barracks, hospital, store, and bakery.

19 buildings remain. 12 structures are original, and 7 others have been reconstructed after archaeological excavations.

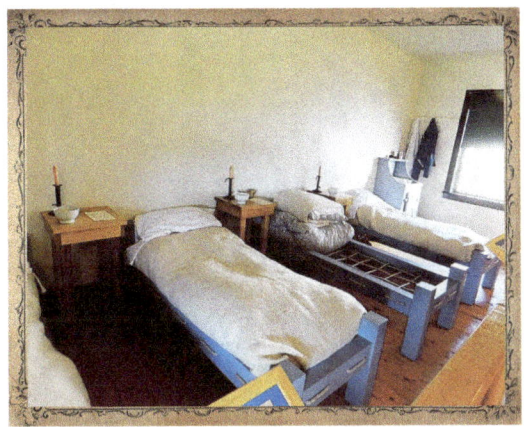

My favorite building is the doctor's office, reconstructed to appear as it did in 1867 to 1870. A doctor's duties included treating the sick, examining recruits, and making daily weather reports.

Don't miss the cemetery, where soldiers were buried with the honor of a drum escort and three-gun salute. The cemetery contains the remains of three men, who died of exposure, delirium, and disease.

The fort was abandoned in 1870.

How to get to Fort Wilkins:

Fort Wilkins is located at 15223 US Hwy 41, near Copper Harbor.

Voices from the past:

"It ain't so much the snow, but the isolation that can be the death of you." **Army laundress.**

"We are greatly troubled for mechanics. I have had to put a shoe on a horse (and) lay brick and plaster with my own hands the same day." **1st Lieutenant William J. Dawes, 1867.**

A word about fort cooking:

Every private had to take a turn at cooking for the company. Officer's would often overlook Army regulations and choose the best soldier for the job, to keep morale high.

*"I attribute much of the sickness created in the Army to insufficient and bad cooking." **Captain John N. King, 1865***

A moment in time:

The sailing vessel, ***John Jacob Astor***, unloaded supplies at Fort Wilkins on September 21, 1844, and the wind changed. A gale caused the ship to break up on the rocks. The entire winter was spent trying to free the ship. Rigging and machinery were saved, but the ship was lost, causing difficulties for the settlements along Lake Superior, including Fort Wilkins. The scattered remains of the ship are near the dock at Fort Wilkins. Today, divers explore the wreck of the John Jacob Astor.

Voices from the past:

"Every assistance was rendered by the officers and men of Fort Wilkins. They kept up fires as nigh the Shore as they could...and watched for us all night, though completely drenched in the rain and by the Surf and Spray flying over them." **Captain Benjamin Stannard, Shipmaster, 1844.**

Fort Michilimackinac

M any flags have flown over *Fort Michilimackinac*, including the white flag of France from 1715, followed by the
British flag in 1761. The fort you see today is a reconstruction
of the British fort of 1778, based on records and archaeological

excavations. Excavations have been going on at the fort for more than 60 years.

Over two million artifacts have been discovered during excavations. One of my favorite pieces is this red stoneware teapot, created in England between 1761 and 1770.

Initially, Fort Michilimackinac was an important part of fur trading between France, which controlled Michigan, and Canada. It became a vital supplier of goods to traders along the Great Lakes.

The French gave up the fort in 1761, when they were defeated in the French and Indian Wars. In 1763, the local Ojibwe killed most of the British within the fort. The Ojibwe were able to control the fort for a year, when it was again taken over by the British.

Groups who lived at the fort included soldiers, traders, and wives of some of the men. They lived in about 30 drafty, poorly built buildings contained within a stockade.

The fort was abandoned in 1781 when a stone fort, Fort Mackinac, was established on Mackinac Island. Many of the buildings and materials were moved to Fort Mackinac.

As you explore the fort, you will come upon the imposing Commanding Officers House. The interior of the house is spacious and comfortable.

You can also visit the priest's house, blacksmith shop, soldier's barracks, and the Church of St. Anne.

How to get to Fort Michilimackinac:

Fort Michilimackinac is located off I-75 in Mackinaw City.

A word about life at the fort:

A brief glimpse of life at the fort comes down to us from a diary kept by surgeon's mate, Daniel Morison, from 1769 to 1772.
The diary describes in detail various acts of violence committed
against him and others. Some of the incidents include assaulting
Morison's cousin with an axe, various beatings with fists, the rape
of a 10 year old girl, adultery, robbery, extortion of money from
the traders, and drunkenness. One man is described as receiving
1000 lashes for desertion, when the customary punishment was
30 lashes.

Old Mackinac Point Lighthouse

The **Old Mackinac Point Lighthouse** began operation in 1889. It housed four generations of lighthouse keepers. The keeper's dwelling was completed in 1892, and was a duplex, with room for two lighthouse keepers and their families.

Inside the keeper's dwelling, you can see the sitting room, complete with a woodstove for frigid Michigan winters.

You can also see the dining room, and the cozy keeper's kitchen, also from 1910.

Don't miss the fascinating shipwreck museum, located in the old warehouse. My favorite artifact within the museum is the brass door key discovered in 2004. It was used to unlock the tower door in case someone was locked in the tower.

Lights on the New Mackinac Bridge or Big Mac, made the lighthouse obsolete and it was closed down in 1957.

How to get to Old Mackinac Point Lighthouse:

The Old Mackinac Point Lighthouse is on the shore of Lake Huron, just off I-75 within the Michilimackinac State Park.

Voices from the past:

A common practice among men of the sea has been to write down messages and place them in bottles or brass tubes. A final crew list and other messages were preserved in case a ship went down. These are some of the recovered words, written long ago:

"Having lashed Vessey to me with heaving line, so will be found together." **J. Sidley, Picton. (Sidley was the owner of the Picton, and Vessey was his 12-year-old son. Their remains were never found)**

"This is terrible. The steamer is breaking up fast. I am aboard from Grand Haven to Chicago." **(a sailor on board the Alpena, which sunk in 1880)**

"October 16, 3 o'clock, on board the Alpena...she has broke her port wheel; is at the mercy of the seas; is half full of water; God help us, Capt. Napier washed overboard. The finder of these note will please communicate with my wife and let her know of my death."

"This is of the Manistee, in a fearful storm. May not live to see morning. Ever yours to the world." **John McKay, Captain. (The Manistee was sunk in 1883, and no remains were ever found)**

"Captain of the steamer Hudson. Steering engine gave out, we are all going. Good-by." **(The Hudson sank in 1901)**

A word about ghost ships:

The ***Griffon***, built in 1679, was a small, single sailed ship. It was meant to be used to carry furs, and for exploration. On August 7, 1679, the ship set sail on her first voyage to Green Bay. There were 32 men on board. Once reaching Green Bay, a large cargo of furs was loaded. She left Green Bay on September 18, with a crew of 6. Bound for Niagara, the ship went missing. Over the centuries, various sightings of the "phantom ship" have been recorded.

Manitoulin island on Lake Huron, offers up some clues as to what might have happened to the missing men. The light keeper on the island reported finding five or six skeletons in a cave, before the turn of the century. One of the skeletons was very large, and it has been reported that the Danish captain was a large Danish man. Old French coins, brass buttons, and two old gold watches were found near the skeletons.

Mackinac Island

L ovely ***Mackinac Island*** is a sublimely beautiful spot on Lake
Huron. Native Americans were living on Mackinac Island
for at least 700 years before Europeans got there. They came to
the island to fish,and named the waters, "the home of the fish."
Artifacts have been found on the island, dating to the Woodland
period, 1000 BC to 1650 AD.

European settlement began in 1670, when Father Claude Dablon started a mission on the island. The mission was moved by Father Jacques Marquette to St. Ignace on the mainland. Around 1708 the mission was moved to what is now Mackinaw City, where French soldiers established Fort Michilimackinac.

Today, visiting Mackinac Island is a trip back in time. In fact, the movie "Somewhere in Time," was filmed there. Automobiles have been banned since 1898. Now the only way to get around is by bicycle or horse-drawn taxi.

One of the most prominent structures on the island is the Grand Hotel, a massive Victorian structure, built in the 1880s. You can also visit the Biddle House, house of Agatha And Edward Biddle, who lived there around 1830.

Strolling through downtown Mackinac is a joy. Streets are lined with quaint Victorian buildings, including the American Fur Company Store, Dr. Beaumont Museum, Benjamin blacksmith shop, and McGulpin House.

How to get to Mackinac Island:

You can take a ferry from Mackinaw City to Mackinac Island, which is located on Lake Huron in between the state's Upper and Lower Peninsulas.

Ghost story:

The Grand Hotel, established in 1887, has a few ghosts. Numerous apparitions have been seen walking down the halls of the Grand Hotel, including soldiers, women in Victorian dress, and a man in a top hat.

Fort Mackinac

M assive *Fort Mackinac,* located on Mackinac Island, was established by the British in 1780, during the American Revolution. The fort's main function was to protect the British fur trade. British occupied the fort up until Americans took control in 1796.

In July 1812, the British captured the fort in the first battle on land of the war of 1812. Treaty negotiations in 1814 led to the island and the fort being given back to the United States.

John Jacob Astor began the American Fur Company and by the 1820s the fur trade was big business. The fort remained active until 1895.

There are 14 structures which are original to the site. The stone officer's quarters, built in 1780, is the oldest building in Michigan.

The post schoolhouse was built in 1879, fulfilling a requirement for all officers and enlisted men to have their children attend school. It was operated through the 1880s.

The busy soldier's canteen of 1889 afforded men the opportunity to play billiards, read magazines, and drink a mug of "Schlitz of Milwaukee" for 5 cents a glass. The post canteen was established so drinking alchoholic beverages could be controlled and regulated.

The all-important post bathhouse, built in 1885, had hot and cold running water, where soldiers could bathe "once a week, or more" said Dr. John Bailey, the post surgeon.

You can also visit the officers stone quarters built in 1780, and the north blockhouse built in 1798. It is one of the oldest buildings at the fort.

The post hospital was built in 1828, and is the oldest standing hospital in Michigan. It houses a fascinating exhibit on military medicine, including a collection of cross sections of human brains.

How to get to Fort Mackinac:

Fort Mackinac is a main feature located on Mackinac Island.

A word about fort medicine:

Bleeding was a common form of treatment, using leeches and other methods to open veins in the arm or neck. Loss of blood was believed to relieve illness and cure disease.

Cupping was another method of treatment. Glass cups were placed on the back or stomach and heated, creating suction and fluid movement to the skin surface.

Blistering caused pain in one area of the body, with the belief that it would reduce pain in another area of the body.

Voices from the past:

"I cut a piece of linen one fourth the size of the abdomen and dipping it into alcohol, spread it evenly on the surface of the abdomen...and then setting it on fire allowed it to burn out. This I repeated." **Charles E. Isaacs, M.D. January 5, 1845.**

"Doc has had a good deal to do lately. Several cases of sickness at the mines. Mrs. Sumner was up and had a tooth out yesterday. She stood it quite well & went off laughing." **Lt. William Dawes, February 19, 1868.**

Ghost story:

No one is sure when burials began in the post cemetery, because there are both British and American soldiers from the War of 1812 buried there. There are 108 burials in the cemetery, only 39 of which are identified. There are several children also buried in the cemetery. The apparition of a woman has been seen, sitting in a corner, perhaps mourning her dead children. The ghost is believed to be the mother of Josiah and Isabel Cowles, who were buried in the cemetery in 1884 and 1888.

To build the stables, the post cemetery had to be moved, but not all of the remains were moved. During construction of the hotel, several skeletons were unearthed, both the skeletons of soldiers and Native Americans. The location of the hotel was also the site of a Native American burial ground. So many skeletons were unearthed, that it was decided to just leave them where they lay, and build over them.

Favorite Places to Camp

F **ayette Historic Park Campground** is lovely. It has a total of 61 sites, all of which have power. There is ample shade and scenery to enjoy. The townsite of Fayette is a short walk from the campground. There are showers, and a swimming beach within the campground. For reservations, call 800-447-2757 or book online by visiting https://midnrreservations.com/

Fort Wilkins State Park Campground is yet another sublimely beautiful campground. There are both an east and west campgrounds, with a total of 159 sites, all with power. The campground has showers, laundry, and easy access to the Fort Wilkins Historic Site. For reservations, call 800-447-2757 or book online by visiting https://midnrreservations.com/

Random Thoughts
What History Means to Me

F irst, let me start by sharing with you my opinion of what history isn't. History is not a collection of random dates, names, and places for you to memorize. History is not a dry and uninteresting class you have to pass to graduate.

I believe history is a tangible thing. You can actually *feel* history in the places you go, and the sights you see. I remember walking up to the Acropolis in Athens. I looked down at the well-worn marble steps and wondered about how many ancient philosophers had climbed these very steps, thousands of years ago.

You don't have to go far away to experience the *feeling* of history. If you are lucky enough to live in an old house, you may experience history in your own surroundings. You might say to yourself, *"If only these walls could talk."*

During my travels across the United States, I *felt* history in many, many places. If you travel across the country like I did, you will *feel* the wonderful history of our beautiful country for yourself, and you will never be the same. You will discover what it means to be an American.

—◦◦◦◦—

Why I travel, and why you should too:

I decided to travel across the country by car because I wanted to rediscover America. When I first set out to explore the history of our country, I wanted to find out why America is the greatest country on earth, and what it means to be an American.

The politics of these United States can be frightening and polarizing. I prefer to focus on what unites us, not what divides us. What unites us is we all live in a spectacularly beautiful country, with warm, wonderful people.

I began my journey five years ago, starting out in my Honda CRV. I soon realized I loved the lifestyle, so now I travel in a small RV. From my small RV, I look out on a country with a unique and colorful, multicultural tapestry, unlike any other country on earth.

I have a degree in Archaeology, and a passion for all things archaeological. I love history, with a side love of paleontology. It is these three passions that I set my trip agenda around. I set out to discover the archaeological sites, history, and paleontological world of our country.

As I travel and write my books, I get asked all the time, especially by women, "What is it like to travel by yourself? Aren't you scared?" The truth is, I believe everyone should do what I did. It's a wonderful way to discover our country, and to rediscover yourself. The truth is, I'm scared not to travel. Traveling allows you to get to know yourself, in ways not possible when sitting on the couch watching TV.

We tend to spend a lot of our lives tuning out the world and our place within it. When you travel, you are quite literally forced to deal with your own thoughts, emotions, and feelings. You can discover yourself while traveling. You can come to understand what makes you who you are, and how you can perhaps become a better person. Above all, traveling gives you mental clarity to figure out how to live with intent. It's a way to guide your life, not just wait for things to happen.

Travel Tips & Stuff

What You Need to Know

How to get started:

P lanning your trip should be one of the most exciting things about it. You want to be spontaneous, but it is also very wise to plan your route, so you can take full advantage of all the time and miles you will invest.

- First, decide your passions. If you love airplanes, trains, or old vehicles, plan your trip around that. If you love gardens or architecture, seek that out as the focus of your trip.

- Next, read and research areas of the country that will let you enjoy what you are interested in.

- Make a list by state and city or town, of what you want to see.

- Take your handy road atlas and locate the areas on the pages.

- Make a tentative route plan, so you have an idea of where you are going.

Travel tip: Avoid trying to plan your trip down to a schedule of days, hours, or minutes. On a road trip, it will be virtually impossible to know where you will be on any given day. If you adhere to a schedule, you are more likely to stress out, and less likely to actually enjoy yourself, which is the whole point.

What you need:

You need to bring along a sense of adventure and a curious mind. You need to ditch the idea of always being on a schedule, and live a little more spontaneously to thoroughly enjoy yourself. Things will happen as you travel, both good things and bad things, and you need to prepare your mind and your soul for day-to-day changes.

So much of our lives are planned out. Between growing up, going to school, finding a career, marriage, kids, or whatever, people have lost much of the ability to be spontaneous. But you must take spontaneity on the trip with you, because you may make detours along the way to see something really spectacular.

So, for the practical stuff you need:

A great vehicle-I am now five years into the trip and have swapped out my Honda CRV for a small RV, just under 20 feet. I go small because I see humongous RVs on the road, towing a car behind, and all I can think of is, they can't go just anywhere. They are too big. Bad gas mileage, cumbersome to drive, slow, and not agile like my small RV. So, I encourage you, if you want to go car or RV camping and be able to go on remote dirt roads, get an agile vehicle, and small RVs are great.

Travel tip: Don't be afraid to do some modifications to your vehicle. I have made many alterations to my RV, including changing the plumbing, which used to be a mere 4 inches off of the ground, so I would break it all the time. It's now encased in my outside storage compartment. I am also a minimalist, so I have jettisoned anything I won't use or don't love. Don't be afraid to get rid of unnecessary stuff.

An awesome camera that you know inside and out. I use a Nikon and it takes wonderful pictures. Don't skimp on a camera, and don't think a cellphone camera is all you need, because you want the best for your beautiful photos.

Window shades-the best ones are magnetic so you just place them against your windows and they cling to them, obscuring the view inside your car. I also have magnetic window screens, so I can leave my windows down with no bugs!

Battery operated fans and lights-these are important, so you don't have to rely on your house batteries for light and cooling options.

Portable air compressor-this little gem plugs into your cigarette lighter and will inflate your tires if you have a flat. Make sure the air compressor can reach to all of your tires, including your rear tires.

Portable battery charger and power bank-mine comes with battery cables and the power bank, yet once inside the case, it is small enough to put in your glove compartment. This little item, unfortunately, I have had to use, and it saved me.

Portable generator-I have two gas powered generators on the back of my RV, which are hooked together with a coupling unit. I have an interior generator, but after much expense and multiple repairs, it still doesn't work. Now I have generators which will run everything, including AC, and I can maintain them myself.

All season clothing-you never know what different states will bring for weather, so take hot weather and cold weather clothes, and a fair amount of shoes appropriate for hiking, or walking, sandals, and slippers, which are nice at night. Also take along a pair of cheap rubber flip-flops to wear in the public showers you might go into.

Your own pillows-I like my own pillows, so I don't wake up with neck cramps, especially after sleeping in the car.

Sleeping bag and cozy blankets-you want to stay warm and layering is everything.

Warm hat, warm socks, and fuzzy jammies to keep you warm for cold nights sleeping in the car.

A great road atlas, and great guidebooks-get one that's easy to read, with great pictures. For a road atlas, just get one that is easy to read.

A word about photography:

Along with a great camera, you need to have a great eye. This is easier than it sounds once you have worked with your camera and are comfortable taking pictures with it. I am not a professional photographer, but I like my pictures and other people do too.

These are my tips for taking great pictures:

- Experiment with taking both horizontal and vertical shots.

- Don't always put the subject of the photo in the middle of the photograph.

- This one is important: pay attention to the foreground, and if possible, have something, a plant or whatever, in the foreground to help give the photo dimension and depth.

- This one is important too: turn around often to see the view you just came from. I do this quite often and some of my best pictures have resulted from when I turned around and took the shot.

You can also take a mental photo. Place an image in your mind that you can call upon later. Use all of your senses to see, hear, smell, and maybe even to taste, what is around you. You have the means to fully experience your surroundings, and that is very important to a traveler. When you take a mental photo, be sure to jot down quick little details about what you saw, heard, smelled, or tasted, so you can jog your memory later.

And last, but not least...don't be posing in front of everything, everywhere, to show that you actually went somewhere. Most people want to see themselves in your photo and be mentally transported there, but they can't if you are there already.

To camp or not to camp:

Car or RV camping is great. I prefer it to sleeping on the cold, hard ground in a tent. I can lock the doors, put my window shades up and be cozy for the night.

Some people camp in a Walmart parking lot and feel safe. I do not. I believe that if you are in a busy area, you are more likely to be confronted by a nut job who may bother you. Nothing against Walmart, and many Walmart stores don't allow overnight parking. I don't go for rest areas either because they have a track record of incidents happening to people in rest areas, especially women travelers.

I have come to love casino parking lots. I enjoy gambling, so for a little money, many casinos will provide overnight stays if you gamble a little inside the casino. I also do a lot of boondocking, because it's free, and I believe you are safer parked out in the middle of nowhere in the dark.

I also enjoy camping in state or national campgrounds, wildlife sanctuaries, and fairgrounds.

A word about safety:

When you are a woman traveling alone, it's critical to keep a low profile. Don't tell people you are traveling alone, where you are staying, or any other personal information.

I don't go to bars or get drunk. I'm not preaching but you are on your own, in a city or town you've never been to, and you don't know anyone, so it's not the time to lose control of what you are doing. When you are in control, you are better able to decide which people you want to get to know better.

Travel tip: If you feel vulnerable traveling alone, that's OK. Vulnerability is part of passion, and traveling is a passionate thing to do. You can put one of those family stickers on your vehicle to indicate to others that you are not traveling alone, which can help you feel more secure.

Maintain your connections:

When you are traveling alone, there is a definite sense of discon-nection. It feels almost like you are the only one in the world, traveling through space and time. That's why it's critical to keep your connections to loved ones active.

Be on Facebook while you are traveling. You may not have internet a lot of the time, or the internet will be poor. Consider paying to have your phone be a hotspot. It's a little bit of money per month, but it's worth it and has saved me from being without internet. I love the convenience of it, and you will too.

Plan your journey around visiting family members or friends you haven't seen for a long time, or people that are good friends. When you see people you know, it will ground you, so you can continue traveling.

Check in by phone with loved ones. They worry about you, and it's good for both of you to stay connected no matter where you are.

Consider traveling with a pet. I now travel with my 12 year-old sheltie Rosie, after losing my beloved sheltie, Sadie. Rosie is a wonderful companion. She is also an excellent watchdog, and barks her head off at other dogs and people.

Travel tip: One of the easiest and best ways I stay connected while traveling is to offer to take a photo for someone I don't know. Many couples, families, or singles would love to have more pictures of themselves traveling. It's an easy and quick way to have a connection with a fellow traveler, and it's good manners too.

Practical matters:

You need to have an address to send your mail to. Keep in touch with whomever is nice enough to do this for you.

You will also need to come back occasionally to register your car, vote, go to doctor visits, and take care of any other business. You can't leave it all behind, as tempting as that may be.

Bad things that happened:

I have had a few problems, mostly associated with my RV. I bought an older model, vintage 1999, and I have had to do a few repairs.

My worst experience came when I took my rig in to a shop in Spokane, Washington (who shall remain nameless.) All I needed was an oil change. I got the oil change and was about an hour south of town on a Friday at 4:30, when my engine blew.

I was in the middle of the eastern Washington prairie, many miles from the nearest town. All I could do was watch my oil drain out onto the Interstate. I can't help but think it was associated with my oil change, but I couldn't prove it. The moral of this story is: DON'T LET JUST ANYONE WORK ON YOUR VEHICLE.

Good things that happened:

I have met many great people on my travels, from all walks of life. I have also learned not to judge people. I have met numerous homeless people who are often just wanting a kind word, and not to be treated like dirt.

People have mistaken me for a homeless person, and I too, have been treated like dirt. When I can, I try to help people and be kind to them. Most of the time, they smile and reciprocate. You will always meet people who are unkind, but they are just as likely to be driving a huge expensive rig, or to be homeless.

We are all Americans, and we are all part of the human race. When you meet people across the country, you realize just how important it is to get to know your fellow citizens, and learn more about how they view the world and our country.

I have to give a special shout-out to the many dedicated people, often volunteers, who staff our state and national parks and monuments. They work tirelessly to ensure the health of our natural resources, and help travelers enjoy their visit. The same is true of the many people who staff the museums in small towns and large cities. They enjoy history, like I do, and it shows in their smiles.

Along with wonderful people, I have seen an America that is spectacularly beautiful, with open prairies, majestic mountains, and crystal clear rivers. I have seen a small fraction of the history of our country. I have seen the memorials to the brave people who shaped our country. I have fallen in love with America in a way that was not possible sitting in my living room. People ask me, "would I do it again?" The answer comes easily, "Yes, in a heartbeat."

Bibliography

America Revealed, LIFE Books, 2012.

Billock, Jennifer, *Ghosts of Michigan's Upper Peninsula*, The History Press, 2018.

Colonial Michilimackinac Map & Schedule, Mackinac Island State Park Commission, 2021.

Fort Mackinac, Mackinac Island State Park Commission, 2021.

Fort Mackinac Map & Schedule, Mackinac Island State Park Commission, 2021.

Greenfield Village Visitor's Map, Henry Ford.

Historic Mackinac Island Visitor's Guide, Mackinac Island State Park Commission, 2013.

Keweenaw National Historical Park, National Park Service, 2021.

Mackinac State Historic Parks, Mackinac Island State Park Commission, 2021.

Morison, Daniel, *The Doctor's Secret Journal*, Mackinac State Historic Parks, 2018.

Old Mackinac Point Lighthouse, Mackinac Island State Park Commission, 2021

Old Mackinac Point Lighthouse Map & Schedule, Mackinac Island State Park Commission, 2021.

Quincy Mine, Keweenaw National Historical Park.

Frederick Stonehouse, *Haunted Lakes*, Lake Superior Publishing, 1997.

Index

Referenced by Sections

D

Dablon, Father Claude-see Mackinac Island

Daniels, Jeff-see Dreams of Michigan

Dawes, Lieutenant William J-see Fort Wilkins, Fort Mackinac

Dayton, Ohio-see Greenfield Village

Delaney, Lucy A.-see Greenfield Village

Dwight Eisenhower's Lincoln-see Henry Ford's Museum of American Innovation

E

Ebmodaakowet, the Archer-see Sanilac Petroglyphs

Edison, Thomas-see Greenfield Village

F

Fayette Historic State Park Campground-see Favorite Places to Camp

Ford, Gerald-see Famous People from Michigan

Ford, Henry-see Famous People from Michigan, Henry Ford's Museum of American Innovation

Ford Motor Company Building-see Greenfield Village

Fort Malden-see River Raisin Battlefield Park

Fort Wilkins Campground-see Favorite Places to Camp

J

Jackson Iron Company-see Fayette Historic State Park

Jeter, Derek-see Dreams of Michigan

John F. Kennedy's Lincoln Continental-see Henry Ford's Museum of American Innovation

John Jacob Astor ship-see Fort Wilkins

K

Keckley, Elizabeth-see Greenfield Village

King, Captain John N. -see Fort Wilkins

L

Lake Michigan-see Fayette Historic State Park

Lake Superior-see Fort Wilkins

Lincoln, Abraham-see Henry Ford's Museum of American Innovation

Lindbergh, Charles-see Famous People from Michigan

M

Madonna-see Famous People from Michigan

Manistee-see Old Mackinac Point Lighthouse

Manitoulin Island-see Old Mackinac Point Lighthouse

Q

Quincy, Massachusetts-see Quincy Mine

R

Red Jacket, Seneca Chief-see Calumet

River Raisin Massacre-see River Raisin National Battlefield Park

S

Shelton House-see Fayette Historic State Park

Sidley, J-see Old Mackinac Point Lighthouse

Sidley, Vessey-see Old Mackinac Point Lighthouse

Somewhere in Time-see Mackinac Island

T

Thomas Edison's Laboratory-see Greenfield Village

Tommyknockers-see Quincy Mine

V

Victoria Mine-see Old Victoria

Victoria Mining Company-see Old Victoria

About the Author

Julie Bettendorf is a world traveler with a degree in archaeology and a background in history. She has traveled extensively throughout Egypt, Central America, South America, Europe, and the United Kingdom, visiting archaeological and historical sites all along the way.

Currently, Julie is traveling around the US visiting ghost towns, ancient rock art sites, and archaeological wonders as part of research for her ongoing historical travel series entitled *Wandering Woman*. Wandering Woman is a set of state-by-state guides, full of photographs, historical anecdotes, and unique tips to help other women travel and explore solo across the US by car or RV. Julie enjoys writing freelance blogs, traveling frequently with her two adult children, and hiking outdoors with her faithful dog companion Rosie.

Also by Julie Bettendorf

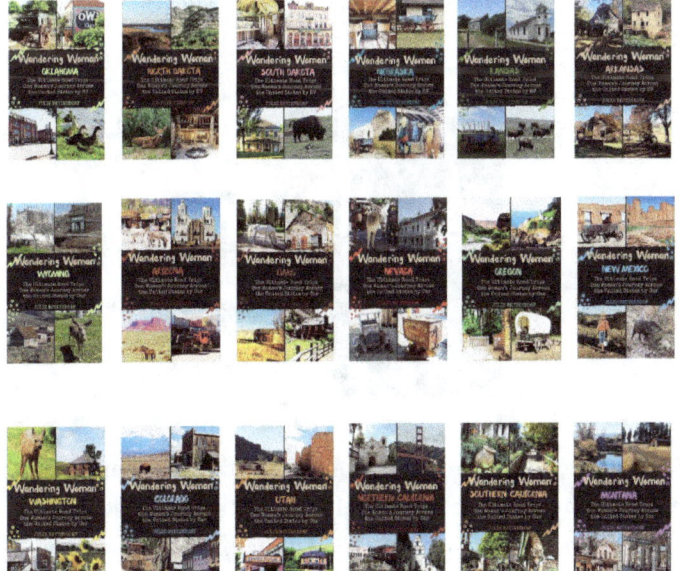

Wandering Woman: Michigan is the most recent book in the ***Wandering Woman Travel Series,*** available in both ebook and paperback.

Julie has published two children's books in an ongoing, beautifully illustrated travel series entitled ***Anthony Ant Goes to France*** and ***Anthony Ant Goes to Egypt***.

She has also published a work of historical fiction entitled ***Luxor: Book of Past Lives*** which has recently been released as an audiobook, read by renowned narrator Barry Shannon.